The Prodigal Prayer Guide

Scripture-Based Prayers for the Prodigal in Your life

Laura Perry, Francine Perry,
AND Carolyn Morgan

Edited by Kendra White

American Family Association
107 Parkgate Drive
Tupelo, Mississippi 38801
www.afa.net

Printed in the United States of America

ISBN 978-1-935932-39-0

Cover design by Canada Burns

Table of Contents

Introduction: Stories of Hope
By Kendra White

God specializes in impossible situations, and He loves to prove that hopeless cases aren't hopeless after all. Never give up. Pray, pray, and keep on praying. Your prayers accomplish more than you have ever dreamed.
— Francine Perry (mother of former prodigal)

Luke 15:11–32 tells the story of the prodigal son and his father. The son demanded his inheritance, left home, and squandered everything he had in reckless living. Meanwhile his loving father never gave up hope that his son would have a change of heart and return home. He stood by, watching and waiting, ready to forgive and ready to embrace.

If you have a prodigal in your life, this is the posture God has called you to take. Stand ready. Be hopeful. Pray.

First Corinthians 13:7 says that love always hopes. No matter how dark the situation may seem, keep praying.

Perhaps you feel too angry and hurt to even think straight, and you don't know what to pray. Maybe you've been staring down the road that leads home for a long time, and you are just so tired of waiting. Whatever your reason for picking up this book, we hope it will equip you to pray and think rightly as you continue interceding for your loved one. Whether your prodigal is a son, daughter, cousin, brother, sister, or friend, God is able to sustain you through this difficult time.

Right now you have an opportunity. In the midst of your grief, God is offering you a beautiful invitation to trust Him and draw nearer to Him than ever before as you eagerly wait for the return of your prodigal.

This *Prodigal Prayer Guide* is filled with powerful, Bible-based* prayers to pray over your loved one as you intercede for him/her by name before the throne of God. These prayers were written by parents of prodigals and former prodigals who have returned to God and right relationship with Him.

But be warned: as you trust the Lord to change the heart of your prodigal, you may find that He changes *your* heart as well.

Many prayers are based on a specific passage of scripture listed in the title, but the language has been paraphrased by the authors in the main body of the prayer. Within each prayer, references are provided only for direct quotations from the Bible.

Meet the Authors Who Wrote
the Prodigal Prayers

Laura Perry was once a prodigal. Although she was raised in a Christian home, Laura became convinced she was "supposed to be male." She walked away from her godly upbringing and began pursuing cross-sex hormones, surgery, and a new life as "Jake." Eventually, she became depressed and tired of the lies. But God had certainly not forgotten her! And neither had her praying mother and father. Jesus rescued her out of the pit of her own sin and has completely transformed and redeemed her life beyond what Laura or her mother,

Francine, ever dreamed possible. Laura has now fully embraced her feminine identity and is engaged to a wonderful man of God, Perry Smalts.

Francine Perry thought her world would crumble when her daughter Laura came out as transgender. But after many years of fasting and praying, as well as a painful process of surrendering her own life fully to

God, Francine witnessed a miracle. Her daughter returned home and into a right relationship with Jesus! Laura has now been faithfully serving the Lord as a woman for many years. She is on staff at First Stone Ministries helping others who struggle with sexuality and gender identity issues.

Inspired by the radical transformation in Laura's life, Francine and the ladies in her Bible study group felt compelled to begin praying for other prodigal children who had walked away from the Lord. That's when they started the Prodigal Prayer Basket. It's nothing fancy—just a basket where anyone can write the name of a prodigal who has strayed from the Lord.

Carolyn Morgan joined Francine's Bible study before Laura's return and by God's design developed a close friendship with Francine. She offered to pray using scripture prayers she had written out of her own desire to see her prodigal and others return to God. Out of this was birthed a  regularly scheduled hour of prayer for all the names in the basket, with Carolyn leading and writing scripture prayers. Having a prodigal of her own, Carolyn saw the great need for corporate intercession for loved ones who have abandoned their faith. Though she is still waiting for her miracle, she and the prayer team have witnessed twenty-two prodigals returning home, and many more are reportedly on the verge of return. They rejoice greatly and praise God every time.

Consider Starting a Prodigal Prayer Basket

You are not alone in this journey, and your loved one is not the only person who has ever strayed from God. Seeing a prodigal walk away from God can feel so isolating and so private. But God designed the body of Christ to thrive with fellowship and encouragement, not isolation.

Consider gathering with other believers and starting a Prodigal Prayer Basket of your own. Most of the prayers in this book are individual prayers designed to pray privately over your loved one. Other prayers, however, are corporate prayers—designed to pray with others over groups of prodigals.

Ever since Francine, Laura, and Carolyn began sharing this idea, many others all over the world have started Prodigal Prayer Baskets. Moms and dads and sisters and brothers are fasting, praying, and believing God for a breakthrough in their prodigals' lives. God is in the business of changing hearts and transforming lives!

Additional Resources

Many prodigals today are specifically struggling with issues related to gender or sexuality. If this applies to your prodigal, please don't go through this alone. There are ministries, support groups, and more resources waiting for you at **inhisimage.movie.**

Personal Prayers for Prodigals

A Prayer for Godly Friends
(Psalm 1 and Galatians 5)

Father, please bless _____ (*name*) with the wisdom and courage to no longer walk in the counsel of the ungodly or stand in the path of those who celebrate sin. At some point in life, he/she began to believe the counsel of the wicked without discernment and began to hang out with sinners and adopt their ways and beliefs. Eventually this led to joining others in scoffing and mocking You and Your Word. Please remove those people from his/her life and replace them with godly people who love You with all their hearts.

I pray that You would give _____ (*name*) a heart that is hungry for You. Turn his/her delights from the desires of the flesh and replace them with a delight for Your Word so that he/she will hunger for it and meditate on it day and night. I know that those who do so will no longer be in a dry, desert land but will be like a tree planted by the rivers of water and yielding good fruit in due season.

May he/she be filled with Your Spirit and begin to demonstrate the fruit of the Spirit. I pray that _____ (*name*) would walk by the Spirit and not gratify the desires of the flesh. For the desires of his/her flesh are against the Spirit, and the desires of the Spirit are against the flesh, for these are opposed to each other and keep _____ (*name*) from doing the things that he/she ought to do.

May _____ (*name*) be led by Your Holy Spirit away from the works of the flesh that are evident in his/her life: sexual immorality, impurity, sensuality, idolatry, sorcery, enmity, strife, jealousy, fits of anger, rivalries, dissensions, divisions, envy, drunkenness, orgies, and such things. For those who do such things will not inherit the kingdom of God, but it is my prayer and desire that _____ (*name*) would receive his/her inheritance in Christ Jesus.

I ask that Your Holy Spirit would fill _____ (*name*) with the fruit of the Spirit: love, joy, peace, patience, kindness, goodness, faithfulness, gentleness, and self-control. May he/she come to saving faith or return to faith in Christ Jesus so that he/she may be able to crucify the flesh with its passions and desires. May he/she live by the Spirit and keep in step with the Spirit.

May You guide him/her away from the wicked who are like chaff which the wind drives away. For I know and grieve that the wicked will not stand in the judgment, nor sinners in the congregation of the righteous, but You, Lord, know the way of the righteous. Please see _____ (*name*) and lead him/her into everlasting life so that he/she will not perish with the wicked.

The Weight of Sin and the Mercy of God
(Lamentations 3)

Lord, I pray for _____ (*name*), who has been led into darkness and not into the light. But I trust that You have a greater purpose. Help him/her to see that this lifestyle is not working out, that it has not led to blessing but to cursing, and that those who walk in darkness will never truly prosper. I pray that the happiness found in sin would become as gravel in his/her teeth and as a bitter drink in the belly. I ask that You would give him/her a longing to return to You and to the joy that You offer.

Lord, I know that_____ (*name*) could never earn Your grace and mercy, and neither could I. But it is because of Your mercies that we are not consumed. Recall this to his/her mind. Remind him/her that those who call upon You in sincerity and humility of heart will be saved. Your mercies are new every morning; great is Your faithfulness. No matter what _____ (*name*) has done, I pray that he/she would know that You can abundantly pardon it. I pray that he/she will say, "The Lord is my portion" and "My soul will hope in You." Help him/her to see that You are good to those who wait for You and to those who seek You.

Lord, You have promised that if we will turn to You, You will not cast us off forever. Bring _____ (*name*) to repentance.

I pray that I will be able to endure seeing him/her make mistakes. I know that You sometimes cause grief in order to make us desperate for You and to humble us. Help me not to interfere but to wait on You. Help me to remember to be compassionate and merciful to those who are leading _____ (*name*) into sin so that I may pray for them also.

Rest in the Valley
(Psalm 23)

Lord, I thank You that You are my Great Shepherd. Help me to wait patiently for You and to follow You. Help me not to run ahead of You as I wait for Your salvation of _____ (*name*), whom I love but whom You love You so much more than I ever could.

Make me lie down in Your green pastures and rest beside the still waters where You will restore my soul. Help me not to get impatient or to worry or fret. Help me to trust fully that You will lead _____ (*name*) back to the fold. You promised that You would leave the 99 to go and find the one lost sheep. He/She is a very lost sheep but is not hidden from You.

Lord, lead me in the paths of righteousness for Your name's sake. Help me to pursue You and love You with all my heart, mind, and soul so that I may one day be ready to receive _____ (*name*) back and to fully forgive. Please transform my heart as well so that I may be a witness and a testimony to him/her.

I confess that this has been a deep, dark valley, even as the Valley of the Shadow of Death for me. At times I have not been sure I could go on. This feels like an insurmountable trial as I have grieved over the things _____ (*name*) is doing. But I choose not to fear, for You are with me. Your rod and Your staff comfort me. Your rod corrects me when my heart sins in worry, doubt, and fear, and Your staff draws me close to Your side and keeps me from going astray myself. Help my heart not to have pride that I am not a lost sheep. Help me not to look down on those who have walked away. Keep me humbly at Your side, praying for those I love.

Even in the midst of this grief, You have prepared a table for me in the midst of this enemy, my grief over my loved one's lifestyle and the brokenness of our relationship. Anoint my head with oil until my cup runs over. May You fill me so completely with Your Holy Spirit that it will flow out of me like a river of living water (John 7:38).

I don't know how long it will take to see the fruit of my prayers, but I trust that You are working even when I cannot see. Though the valley is dark, You are guiding me. Surely goodness and mercy shall follow me all the days of my life. Lord grant to me and to _____ (*name*) that we will dwell together in the house of the Lord forever.

Truth Revealed

(Romans 1:18–32)

O Lord, _____ (*name*) has turned away from You. I know You already know this because You know him/her more completely and intimately than I ever could. But my heart is broken. He/She has suppressed the truth through wickedness and is living a life contrary to Your Word rather than living by faith. I believe that _____ (*name*) knows the truth deep down because You have revealed Yourself in some way at some point, but he/she is not glorifying You as God or giving thanks to You.

I believe that _____ (*name*) has been hurt by _____ (*something/someone that has caused him/her to turn away*) but has blamed and rejected You. He/she has claimed to be wise yet has become foolish, worshipping himself/herself instead of You. Lord, have mercy and compassion on _____ (*name*)! Protect him/her from the lies of the enemy and this culture. Help him/her not to be given over to shameful lusts and unnatural desires.

Remind _____ (*name*) of the truth and heal his/her reprobate mind. Give him/her a hunger for truth and righteousness. Make sin like sand in the mouth so that it would be something _____ (*name*) would want to spit out rather than consume.

Lord, _____ (*name*) has not wanted to retain You in his/her thoughts but has suppressed the truth and pushed You out completely. Father, I pray that You would draw _____ (*name*) back unto Yourself and that rather than being filled with all manner of wickedness and unrighteousness, he/she would be filled with a desire for righteousness and light. I pray that he/she would no longer have pleasure in those who celebrate sin but would tire of the parties and the lies. I pray that You would bring a godly person who loves You into his/her life. Jesus, give _____ (*name*) a desire to be around that person rather than the friends who drag him/her down.

I pray for myself, Lord, that You will keep me thankful, no matter what I am going through. It was an ungrateful heart that led to rebellion (Romans 1:21). Help me to never be unthankful, even in this trial. Keep me humble and focused on You and not on the problem, for You alone are the solution and my sole focus.

A Humble Heart
(Isaiah 26)

Lord, open the gates of _____'s (*name*) heart so that righteous truth will enter in. Keep me in perfect peace and keep my heart and mind stayed on You as I continue to pray for him/her. Help me to trust You, for in Your name is everlasting strength.

Lord, bring _____'s (*name*) heart down and humble him/her. May his/her soul desire You in the night and hunger to seek You early in the morning. I pray that You will bring something into _____'s (*name*) life that will cause him/her to behold the majesty of the Lord.

A Surrendered Heart

(Romans 8:28–29, Psalm 103, II Chronicles 16:9)

Father, I praise You because You have shown Yourself faithful in the midst of a dark valley. I thank You that nothing can separate me from your love. Help me to view this trial as a way for You to grow and mature me! O Lord, use this to conform me to the image of Your Son, Jesus! Help me to humbly surrender my heart fully to You and thus experience a deeper relationship with You than ever before.

Father, I pray that the change I desire to see in _____ (*name*) would first be seen in my life. When _____ (*name*) looks at me, may he/she see a life completely surrendered to you. I know that unless I allow this process to draw me closer to you, it will just make me bitter and hardened.

Father, I thank you for bringing me to a place of humility before You. Humility actually clothes me with the beauty of Jesus Christ. It seems like a paradox, but humility before You brings me joy. Thank you for the truth experienced in my life. When I humbled myself before You, You raised me up.

Bless the LORD, *O my soul,*
and all that is within me,
bless his holy name!
Bless the LORD, *O my soul,*
and forget not all his benefits,
who forgives all your iniquity,
who heals all your diseases,
who redeems your life from the pit,
who crowns you with steadfast love and mercy,
 who satisfies you with good
so that your youth is renewed like the eagle's.
(Psalm 103:1–5)

How could I not praise You? You have forgiven me and redeemed my life from destruction. I marvel at Your grace and mercy. With a humble and contrite heart, I stand in awe of You.

Father, I come to you and confess my wrongful attitude concerning my prodigal. Forgive me for crying out to You to take this nightmare away from my life. Forgive me for my careless words, "Why me? Why my family?" I now realize that You are using my prodigal for my good. You use trials and tests to grow me and mature me. Your desire is for me to finish the race of faith and hear "well done." O God, that is the desire of my heart. II Chronicles 16:9 says, "For the eyes of the LORD run to and fro throughout the whole earth, to give strong support to those whose heart is blameless toward him."

Father, thank you for changing my attitude. May my heart be totally devoted to you. I praise You for working mightily on my behalf.

Peace for the Anxious
(Philippians 4:6–8)

Lord, help _____ (*name*) to no longer be anxious and fearful but instead to turn to You. Take his/her heart of selfish ingratitude and replace it with a desire to be content and satisfied in You. Show him/her that the things of this world have not brought peace but torment.

Help him/her to pray about everything and to present personal petitions to You with thanksgiving. Convict his/her heart of sin because we know that You hear the prayers of the righteous, not the rebellious. Give him/her a heart that desires Your peace, which passes all understanding. Please help _____ (*name*) to no longer focus on evil things but to set his/her heart and mind on the things of You that are true, honest, just, pure, lovely, of good report, virtuous, and worthy of praise.

Desire for the Word of God
(Psalm 119)

Lord, I pray that _____ (*name*) would no longer be defiled in the way but would walk in the law of the Lord. Open his/her eyes to see that he/she would be blessed if he/she would keep Your testimonies and seek You with a whole heart. Show him/her that those who walk in Your ways have great joy and he/she does not. Help _____ (*name*) to see that what appears to bring freedom and happiness has really led to depression and dissatisfaction with life.

Direct his/her heart to seek You and to keep Your statutes because we know that those who desire righteousness will not be ashamed any longer. Give him/her a desire to be clean and no longer covered in the filth of sin. Instead, help _____ (*name*) to see that he/she can be cleansed by turning to Jesus Christ and by following Your Word in repentance.

Give _____ (*name*) such a desire for You that he/she would seek You with a whole heart and not wander from Your commandments anymore. Give him/her such a hunger for Your Word that nothing else will satisfy. Recall to his/her mind scriptures memorized or heard earlier in life so that he/she may no longer desire to sin against You. Bring conviction to his/her heart when considering the evil he/she has engaged in.

Help him/her to meditate on Your Word and to delight in Your statutes. Bring it across his/her path and recall it to mind.

Longing for Home and Wholeness
(Psalm 107)

Lord, I give thanks to You because You are good. No matter what my circumstances look like, I praise You and thank You, for Your mercy endures forever.

Lord, I pray that one day _____ (*name*) would be among the redeemed and that he/she would tell his/her testimony far and wide of how Jesus frees and redeems His children the from the hand of the enemy.

_____ (*name*) may be wandering in the wilderness today, but I trust that You will lead him/her home. Block the entrance to any wicked place in life he/she might find to dwell so that he/she would continue to wander until overcome by a longing for home. Remove his/her hunger and thirst for sin and the empty things of this world and make him/her thirsty for You. Put a longing in his/her heart for home and for Your presence. Lead him/her to Your banqueting table and put over him/her a banner of love (Song of Solomon 2:4).

Help_____ (*name*) to humbly cry out to You for deliverance in times of trouble and distress. Lead him/her forth by the right way and into the city where Your children dwell in peace, in Your house and in Your presence.

Help him/her to be thankful for something You have done in his/her life and to see clearly that it was You who has done this thing. Satisfy his/her longing soul with Your goodness. He/She has been sitting in darkness and has been bound in the afflictions and chains of the enemy. Help him/her to see that it was his/her own rebellion that led to this place. Help him/her to see the fruit of these choices and how it has not been what it was promised to be. May _____ (*name*) see the folly of his/her ways and no longer think that Your Word is foolish.

Bring down _____'s (*name*) heart and humble him/her until there is no one left to help but You, for You indeed are our only hope of salvation. Help _____ (*name*) to love You with all his/her heart, mind, and soul. Bring him/her out of darkness and the shadow of death and break his/her chains. Break the bars of iron that hold him/her captive.

Lord, send Your Word and heal _____ (*name*). Deliver him/her from destruction so that he/she will sacrifice to You the sacrifices of thanksgiving and no longer worship at the altar of self. Help him/her to see Your wonderful works and to praise You. Help him/her to see that You will calm the storm of life and give peace to those who turn to You. Prepare the way ahead of him/her so that one day he/she will exalt You and praise You for Your wonderful works.

I pray for myself, Lord, that You would bring me out of my trouble and deliver me from the torment of my broken heart for _____ (*name*). Help me to focus on You, not on this storm in my life. Help me to see Your works and Your wonders even in the midst of this trial. Keep me safe in the midst of this storm and help me to walk on water as Peter did, with his eyes fixed on You. Help me not to fear the storm that is raging around me but just to keep walking.

Lord, help me to exalt You to others and praise You for the wonderful work You are doing in me. Though for a season my rivers were turned into wilderness and my water springs into dry ground, now, O Lord, turn my wilderness into standing water and my dry ground into springs. Make my hungry soul to dwell here even in the wilderness where You have provided water for my thirsty soul. Help me to sow the fields and plant vineyards that may yield much fruit. Help me to be focused on the work You have for me here so that I may bear much fruit. Lord, do a mighty work in both me and _____ (*name*) so that the righteous shall see it and rejoice and help him/her to understand the lovingkindness of the Lord.

Hope for the Downcast Soul
(Psalm 43)

Lord, I pray for _____ (*name*), who is lost in darkness and living among an ungodly people who are deceitful and unjust. Don't cast him/her off forever. Have mercy, O Lord. Help him/her to see the oppression of the enemy and how the "freedom" he promised has actually led to bondage. Help him/her to see that those who choose sin become slaves to sin (John 8:34).

O Lord, send out Thy light and Thy truth to guide _____ (*name*) back to You. Bring him/her back to Your tabernacle to dwell with You. Bring him/her to Your altar in humility. Remind him/her of the joy seen in other Christians when they praise You. Give him/her a longing for that kind of joy to praise and worship You.

Lord, help my soul not to be downcast as I wait for the salvation of my loved one, _____ (*name*). Why is my soul so downcast? I will speak to my soul and say, "Hope in God." I choose to praise You, Lord, and to hope in You. You are the health of my countenance. You are my God. You will not fail me. You will sustain me.

The Fear of the Lord
(Psalm 34)

Lord, I pray that You will put someone in
_____'s (*name*) life who will magnify You,
exalt Your name, and tell of Your wonderful works in
their life! May their testimony have a huge impact on
_____'s (*name*) heart so that he/she will turn and
seek You.

I know that those who look to You are radiant;
their faces are never covered with shame. So please help
_____ (*name*) to look to You alone as the one who
can remove shame. Hear his/her cries in the night, Lord,
when life isn't working out the way he/she thought. Take
pity, O Lord!

Because the fear of the Lord is the beginning of
wisdom, cause _____ (*name*) to have a healthy
fear of You (Psalm 111:10). Only then will You send Your
angels to encamp around him/her and deliver him/her.

O Lord, allow _____ (*name*) to taste and see
that You are good and to know that there is great blessing
for those who trust in You! Help _____ (*name*) to
see that his/her soul is like a hungry young lion that can
never be satisfied but that those who seek You with their
whole hearts will not lack any good thing.

Help him/her to come and listen to You and obey You.
Teach him/her the fear of the Lord and to desire life, not

death and destruction. Help him/her to see that sin has not brought life and freedom.

Help _____ (*name*) to desire to depart from evil and do good and to seek peace. We know that Your eyes are on the righteous and Your ears are attentive to their cry but You are against those who do evil. So help _____ (*name*) to choose to put on Your righteousness (Ephesians 4:24).

I thank You, Lord, that You are close to the brokenhearted and You save those who are crushed in spirit. My heart is so broken over the sin of _____ (*name*), but help me to remember that You are near!

The Fight for My Prodigal
(Psalm 18)

Lord, I ask that You would fight for _____ (name), who has been deceived by the devil's lies. I know that he/she has chosen to rebel and has embraced a life of sin, but I ask for mercy. Lord, help him/her to remember that You are his/her rock, fortress, deliverer, and God and that You are the only one in whom he/she can truly trust. Help him/her to remember that You are his/her shield, salvation, and high tower.

Lord remind _____ (name) that he/she can call upon You and turn to You with all his/her heart, mind, and soul. Save him/her from enemies. When he/she is afraid, turn his/her heart toward You. May he/she call upon You in distress, and I pray that You would hear! I pray that You would fight for him/her. Take vengeance on the enemy on his/her behalf. And may _____ (name) see the ways You are pursuing and fighting for him/her and be overwhelmed by Your steadfast love!

When David called upon You, the earth shook and trembled, smoke went out of Your nostrils, and fire went out of Your mouth. You bowed the heavens and came down, and You rode upon a cherub to defend him and rescue him. Lord, I pray that You would do the same for _____ (name) and that You would slay the enemy on his/her behalf. I know that he/she has sinned greatly against You, and so have I. But You had mercy on me and took pity on me when I did not deserve it. Do the same for my loved one, I pray.

Lord, You are the living God, and vengeance belongs to you alone. You will subdue the enemies of life under Your feet. Lift _____ (*name*) up above those who want to destroy (him/her.) Lift _____ (*name*) out of the flood. I give thanks to You, even among the heathen. I look forward to the day I will tell them of Your wonderful works and how You rescued and redeemed _____ (*name*). You will give great deliverance, and we will sing praises to Your name.

My Shield and Sustainer
(Psalm 3–4)

You, O Lord, are a shield about me, my glory, and the lifter of my head.

I cry aloud to the Lord, and He answers me from His holy hill. Be a shield around_____ (*name*) and lift his/her head so that he/she may rise from the pit of sin.

Answer me when I call, O God of my righteousness! You have given me relief when I was in distress. Be gracious to me and hear my prayer! How long will _____ (*name*) love vain words, seek after lies, and remain deceived? You set the godly apart for Yourself. I ask that You draw_____ (*name*) and set him/her apart from the world. Thank You for hearing me when I call.

Sometimes I am angry in my grief. Give me the grace I need so that I would not sin against You or those I love. I offer up a sacrifice of praise and put my trust in You.

Lift up the light of Your face upon me and upon _____ (*name*), O Lord! You alone, O Lord, can fill my heart with joy so that I may lie down in peace and sleep in safety. Thank You that because of my faith and trust in You I can lie down and sleep and then arise to serve You another day, for You sustain me. Salvation belongs to the Lord; Your blessing be on Your people! Selah.

Refuge for the Distressed
(Psalm 31)

Father, I lift up _____ (*name*). May he/she take refuge in You and never be put to shame. May Your righteousness deliver him/her. Incline Your ear to _____ (*name*) and rescue him/her speedily! Be a rock of refuge for him/her, a strong saving fortress. May You be his/her rock and fortress as You are mine.

For Your name's sake, You lead me and guide me. May You do the same for _____ (*name*). Take him/her out of the net the enemy has hidden, for You are our refuge. Into Your hand I commit his/her spirit. Redeem him/her, O Lord, faithful God.

I pray that _____ (*name*) would hate those who pay regard to the worthless idols of this world. May he/she trust in the Lord. I will rejoice and be glad in Your steadfast love because You have seen my affliction; You have known the distress of my soul. May You deliver _____ (*name*) from the hand of the enemy and set his/her feet in a broad place.

Be gracious to me, O Lord, for I am in distress; my eye is wasted from grief; my soul and my body also. For my life is spent with sorrow, and my years with sighing; my strength fails because of my iniquity and because of my grief for_____ (*name*). But I trust in You, O Lord. I say, "You are my God."

My times are in Your hand. You have numbered my days and the days of _____ (*name*). Rescue him/her from the hand of the enemy. Make Your face shine on Your servant; save him/her in Your steadfast love! O Lord, let me not be put to shame, for I call upon You. The wicked will be put to shame, but spare _____ (*name*) from going silently to Sheol.

Oh, how abundant is Your goodness, which You have stored up for those who fear You and worked for those who take refuge in You, in the sight of the children of mankind! In the cover of Your presence, You hide them from the plots of men; You store them in Your shelter from the strife of tongues.

Blessed be the Lord, for He has wondrously shown His steadfast love to me when I was besieged and distressed. But He heard the voice of my pleas for mercy for _____ (*name*) when I cried to Him for help.

Love the Lord, all you his saints! The Lord preserves the faithful but abundantly repays the one who acts in pride. Be strong, and let your heart take courage, all you who wait for the Lord!

Admission of Sin
(Psalm 51)

Have mercy on me and those I love, O God, according to Your steadfast love. According to Your abundant mercy, reveal to _____ (*name*) Your righteousness and holiness so that he/she may long for You to blot out all transgressions. May _____ (*name*) feel the uncleanness of his/her heart and seek You so that You would wash him/her thoroughly from iniquity and cleanse him/her from sin.

May _____ (*name*) see his/her transgressions and realize that it is against You, You only, he/she has sinned and done what is evil in Your sight. Help _____ (*name*) to see that he/she was brought forth in iniquity and has a sin nature. May he/she see that You delight in truth in the inward being and that You can teach wisdom in the secret heart.

Purge _____ (*name*) with hyssop that he/she may be clean; wash him/her that he/she may be whiter than snow. Let him/her hear joy and gladness; let the bones that You have broken rejoice. Hide Your face from his/her sins and blot out all his/her iniquities.

Create in _____ (*name*) a clean heart, O God, and renew a right spirit within him/her. Cast him/her not away from Your presence and take not Your Holy Spirit from _____ (*name*). Restore to him/her the joy of

Your salvation and uphold him/her with a willing spirit. Then may _____ (*name*) teach transgressors Your ways, and sinners will return to You.

Deliver us all from bloodguiltiness, O God of our salvation, so that our tongues will sing aloud of Your righteousness. O Lord, open our lips, and our mouths will declare Your praise. For You will not delight in sacrifice, or we would give it; You will not be pleased with a burnt offering. The sacrifices of God are a broken spirit; a broken and contrite heart, O God, You will not despise. This is my prayer for _____ (*name*) and for myself.

The Path to Joy
(Psalm 32:5–11)

Lord, we see in Psalm 32 a beautiful progression that leads to joy and ultimate reconciliation. It begins with acknowledging our sin and seeking forgiveness:

I acknowledged my sin to You, and I did not cover my iniquity; I said, "I will confess my transgressions to the LORD," and You forgave the iniquity of my sin (Psalm 32:5).

Father, I ask in the name of Jesus for myself and _____ (*name*). Help us both see and acknowledge our sin rather than try to hide it. Help us to willingly confess our sins to You so that we may be found by You and receive Your forgiveness.

Then, we read that You lead us to pray for deliverance and preservation:

Therefore let everyone who is godly offer prayer to you at a time when you may be found; surely in the rush of great waters, they shall not reach him. You are a hiding place for me; you preserve me from trouble; you surround me with shouts of deliverance (Psalm 32:6–7).

May You be a hiding place for both me and _____ (*name*). We both need You to preserve us from trouble and to give us Your protection and deliverance. Lord, protect_____ (*name*) from the attacks of the enemy and surround him/her with Your shouts of deliverance.

After we have acknowledged sin, sought forgiveness, and prayed for deliverance and preservation, You promise to instruct us and teach us:

> *I will instruct you and teach you in the way you should go; I will counsel you with my eye upon you. Be not like a horse or a mule, without understanding, which must be curbed with bit and bridle, or it will not stay near you* (Psalm 32:8–9).

Instruct us and teach us in the way we should go. Counsel us both with Your eyes upon us. Give us Your grace so that we would not be stubborn like a horse or mule without understanding. Forgive us when we are stubborn and soften our hearts so that we will embrace Your correction.

Lastly, Your Word tells us to praise You:

> *Many are the sorrows of the wicked, but steadfast love surrounds the one who trusts in the LORD. Be glad in*

the LORD, *and rejoice, O righteous, and shout for joy,*
all you upright in heart! (Psalm 32:10–11)

May Your steadfast love surround us as we trust in
You. We will be glad in the Lord and rejoice and shout
for joy because You have made us upright in heart!

Corporate Prayers for Prodigals

The Tabernacle Prayer
(Hebrews 9 & 10)

Father, we have offered up our sacrifice of praise. We thank You, our holy and awesome God, that You delight to inhabit our praise and to dwell with us. You are Immanuel, God with us. Because of the finished work of Christ, our great High Priest, we draw near with full assurance of faith. We are holding fast our confession of faith and our hope in You without wavering, for we know that You are faithful. Our confidence is not in ourselves but in You.

But who are we, that we should be able come before You? For we are strangers before You and sojourners, a peculiar people. Yet You have called us a chosen race, a royal priesthood, a holy nation, a people for Your own possession. Once we were not a people, but now we are Your people; once we had not received mercy, but now we have received mercy.

We bring the names of all these loved ones before You. Our hearts yearn for them, but You long for them to have hearts that fear You and keep Your commandments. That is our cry also. You know each name in our prayer basket. Each one is precious in Your sight. We call upon the Captain of the host of the Lord to lead us in battle, for we are facing an enemy that we cannot fight on our own. Guide us as we pray and bear witness to the beauty of Your holiness.

Your tabernacle was a beautiful picture of Your holiness and the requirements to enter Your presence. Each part points to Jesus Christ, our great High Priest.

The white linen walls represent Your holiness and remind us that our sin separates us from You. We ask on behalf of our prodigals that You would open their eyes to their sin. Pour out Your kindness and grace on them so that they may be led to repentance. Help them to see that the only way to forgiveness and into Your presence is through Jesus Christ, the only door. He truly is the only way. He is the Truth; He is the Life.

Many of these prodigals were raised in the faith, but some may never have known You. Take the blinders of deception off their eyes and soften their hearts toward You. Help them to realize that a sacrifice has to be made to atone for sin. Through His sacrifice, Jesus became our High Priest who abides forever and is able to save forever those who draw near to God through Him. Draw them near, O God.

The bronze laver reminds us that washing is a daily necessity. We ask that You would wash us clean by Your Word and Your Spirit. See if there is any offensive way within us and lead us according to Your Word. Our prodigals need the washing and cleansing that comes through salvation and then in day-to-day life. This comes only by the working of Your Spirit, not by our might or power. We ask that the Word that was entrusted to them when they were young would burn like fire in their bones and fulfill the purpose for which You sent it.

The golden lampstand was always giving light in the Holy Place. May Jesus bring His light into the darkness of our prodigals' lives and transfer them from the kingdom of darkness into the kingdom of light. May they someday proclaim the excellencies of Him who called them out of darkness into Your marvelous light.

The table of showbread reminds us that Jesus is the bread of life, our daily bread. May our prodigals hunger for that bread, for truth, and for righteousness. May their souls long for Your salvation and may Your words be sweeter than honey to their mouths. May they no longer be satisfied by this world but find true fulfillment only in You. May Your commandments be their delight.

Dear Father, we bring our prayers and praise as sweet offerings to You. We can't begin to express our full gratitude for the privilege of coming through the veil of Jesus' flesh and into Your presence. He poured His blood on the mercy seat and is Himself the mercy seat. Thank You for His sacrifice to redeem us and thank You for all that You will do in answer to our prayers for our prodigals.

May Your resurrection power be at work in and through us and them. It is only that power that can break the strongholds in their lives. Today we have ordered our prayer toward You, and we eagerly watch and wait on the God of our salvation. Our hope is in You. May our souls be anchored by faith and trust in You. We pray in the name of Jesus and for His glory. Amen!

The 10 Commandments Prayer
(Exodus 20)

Now we know that whatever the law says it speaks to those who are under the law, so that every mouth may be stopped, and the whole world may be held accountable to God. For by works of the law no human being will be justified in his sight, since through the law comes knowledge of sin (Romans 3:19–20).

If we say we have no sin, we deceive ourselves, and the truth is not in us. If we confess our sins, he is faithful and just to forgive us our sins and to cleanse us from all unrighteousness. If we say we have not sinned, we make him a liar, and his word is not in us (1 John 1:8–10).

Search me, O God, and know my heart! Try me and know my thoughts! And see if there be any grievous way in me, and lead me in the way everlasting! (Psalm 139:23–24)

1st COMMANDMENT
You shall have no other gods before me.

You alone, O God, are worthy of our praise and adoration, yet we and our loved ones so easily reduce Your worth and esteem ourselves instead. Our prodigals live and act as if You do not exist, and they do not realize that they have made themselves into their own gods. Open their eyes to Your existence and very real presence in this world and in their lives. May the eyes of their hearts be enlightened to know Your love. May the blinders be taken off their eyes. May they be brought out of the darkness and into the light so that they may see You and learn to fear You.

2nd COMMANDMENT

You shall not make for yourself a carved image, or any likeness of anything that is in heaven above, or that is in the earth beneath, or that is in the water under the earth. You shall not bow down to them or serve them, for I the LORD your God am a jealous God, visiting the iniquity of the fathers on the children to the third and the fourth generation of those who hate me, but showing steadfast love to thousands of those who love me and keep my commandments.

Father, we are all guilty of making the things of this world into idols. Anything we treasure more than You is an idol. Our prodigals have elevated the things of this world to the level of idolatry without being aware of this sin. They want to remake You into an image that they have created and that is acceptable in their own eyes. They add to and take away from Your Word to satisfy their own ideas of justice, mercy, and love. They have forgotten that in the judgment of sin, You are merciful through Jesus Christ. Wake them up, Lord, and remind them that You are jealous for their love and devotion. Remind them that the consequences for sin are significant and reverberate down through the generations. Open their eyes to see the spiritual warfare around them so that they may understand that the idols they worship are from the pits of hell. They need to see evil for what it truly is, and they need to see their sin and the sin of those around them. May the facades that they put up drop so that they may see the illusion of their own righteousness and admit their sin. Knock down the idols of their lives so that their hearts may be broken and sorrowful to the point of repentance.

3rd COMMANDMENT
You shall not take the name of the LORD your God in vain, for the LORD will not hold him guiltless who takes his name in vain.

The name of Jesus is above all names, but His name and Your Word are trampled in the streets. Our prodigals do not revere Your Holy name. Some claim Your name and live in sin, believing that You accept them and their sin. We pray that they will be brought to their knees before You in this life and will not be counted among those who are forced to bow before You in the next. Convict their spirits of the offense they cause Your Holy Spirit by their words, behavior, and attitudes. Help them to humble themselves before You so that You do not need to step in and bring humility to them.

4th COMMANDMENT

Remember the Sabbath day, to keep it holy. Six days you shall labor, and do all your work, but the seventh day is a Sabbath to the LORD your God. On it you shall not do any work, you, or your son, or your daughter, your male servant, or your female servant, or your livestock, or the sojourner who is within your gates. For in six days the LORD made heaven and earth, the sea, and all that is in them, and rested on the seventh day. Therefore the LORD blessed the Sabbath day and made it holy.

Dear Father, our children have rejected You in the way that they order their lives. Many no longer attend church and or participate in the body of believers. They have accepted the view of the secular world that Sunday is just another work or leisure day. In doing so, they also reject You as their Creator and reject Your authority and sovereignty over their lives. And they reject Your power in the resurrection that works in and through us. But we rejoice in that power! It is able to do immeasurably more we think or ask! We are so grateful for the fellowship we have among believers and the joy and comfort we have as we come together to study Your Word and to pray. May You give our children a leanness in their souls so that they feel this loss of fellowship. May they feel a hunger in their souls that cannot be satisfied by anything in this world. We ask that their relationships would not satisfy their longings for fellowship. May they truly hunger and thirst for truth and righteousness.

5th COMMANDMENT
Honor your father and your mother, that your days may be long in the land that the LORD *your God is giving you.*

Oh, how our hearts ache for our children! But You long for them so much more. You desire for them to give You honor and praise and to follow in Your ways. We know that in following You, they will learn to give respect and honor and love to their parents. We ask that You would draw their hearts back to Yours; and we trust that in doing so, their hearts would also be drawn back to us. May relationships be restored and forgiveness be granted all around. May we all have hearts full of mercy for them and be ever watching and waiting so that we may rejoice at their return.

6th COMMANDMENT
You shall not murder.

Dear Jesus, you equate murder with a heart full of hatred and anger. Many of these prodigals fall into that category. Only You know what is in in the heart of man. Search their hearts and show them the evil and deception that reside within. Show them how their sin has led them to believe the lies of the world. Break through their hard hearts and bring them to the point of hating their own sin. May the balm of Gilead be poured out on the wounds of their hearts to bring healing and restoration.

7th COMMANDMENT
You shall not commit adultery.

Again, Lord, we go to the words of Jesus, who equated lust in the heart with adultery. Your Word tells us that our hearts are wicked and deceitful above all else and that out of our hearts flow evil thoughts, murder, adultery, fornication, theft, lies, and blasphemies and that these things defile a person.

Lord, we know that the hearts of our prodigals are full of all manner of wickedness and that their own sin deceives them and hardens their hearts. Sin has so altered their thinking that they do not even know they are deceived. They have stopped looking to Christ and all they have been taught of Him. Unbelief has replaced whatever faith they once had. We grieve for them and know that their hard hearts provoke You.

So we ask You to have mercy on them and to open the eyes of their hearts and show them their sin. Take the blinders off their eyes so that they may see Your holiness in contrast to their sin. Soften their hearts to receive Your grace and help. Satan continually sows seeds of deception and temptation, and they fall prey to his snares. Their only hope is in Your protection, revelation, and deliverance. Only You can show them that sin will never deliver what it promises and that it brings long-lasting consequences. Father, our hope is in You. Even our hope for our prodigals rests completely in You. Fill us with Your Spirit so that we may be empowered to live not according to our flesh but in the power of Your Spirit so that we can demonstrate to our prodigals the power of a changed life.

8th COMMANDMENT
You shall not steal.

Theft also flows out of the wicked heart. You are our Creator and Provider. All good gifts come from You. You have given us this world in which we live and have given us work to do that has purpose and value. Those who steal do not value Your provision and the work You have given them to do. They are ungrateful and look only to themselves or the world. Some steal possessions from others, and we pray that You would enable them to steal no longer but to do honest labor and provide for themselves and their own households.

Some steal time, energy, and emotions and are a drain on those around them. We ask that You would fill them up to the fullness of God so that they would not exhaust the people around them but instead replenish and refresh them.

Others steal Your glory, boasting only in themselves. They worship the creatures and the creation rather than their Creator. They have made themselves to be their own gods fashioned in their own image, so they glorify themselves. May You open the eyes of their hearts to see themselves as they truly are. Only then can they repent and see You in all Your glory and holiness.

May they learn to be dependent on You and grateful for all Your provision. We pray that in whatever way our prodigals are stealing, they may be renewed in mind and soul to be able to give to others rather than be takers. May they generously give their lives and love to others.

9th COMMANDMENT
You shall not bear false witness against your neighbor.

Bearing false witness is lying about something or refusing to say what we know to be true to help someone.

It is being deceitful in the way we live. It is the nature of our old self, the nature of Satan. He is the great deceiver. Our prodigals follow after his deceptive ways. We too can fall into this trap since our sinful nature is naturally deceptive. We need truth to be made manifest in our minds and hearts. Our prodigals need to be washed and renewed in spirit and soul. We all must lay aside falsehood and speak truth to one another.

Help us to lay aside the old garment that would lie and bear false witness. Help us to be transparent in our weaknesses in order that we may encourage one another and pray for one another. Help us to be filled with the goodness and truthfulness of Your Spirit so that our lives may demonstrate love, joy, peace, patience, kindness, goodness, faithfulness, gentleness, and self-control. May the kindness of Your Spirit lead our prodigals to repentance. May we all walk in truth, for Your Word is truth.

10th COMMANDMENT
You shall not covet.

Paul admits in Romans 7 that he would not have known what it was to covet apart from the law, but sin seized the opportunity and produced in him all manner of covetousness. Our fleshly nature is bound up with sin. We cannot escape it apart from the power of God. We and our prodigals covet or lust for things that are not ours to have or are not God's design for us. This sinful nature ruins relationships. Father, may our prodigals come face to face with the ugliness of their sinful nature, which is manifested in all of these sins and more. Strip them of their self-sufficiency, their complacency, and especially their self-righteousness. Help them to see that they are helpless to live up to even their own ideas of goodness and righteousness. Bring them to the end of themselves so that their lives may start anew in Christ.

And Father, bring us to the end of ourselves. May we have the grace we need to submit ourselves to You so that we may be filled up with You and have the nature of Christ manifested in our flesh. We try to live up to Your standards, but we are totally inadequate. Help us to live out the love of God without hypocrisy. Help us to love one another within the body of Christ, to love our families and prodigals, and to love those whom You bring into our circle of influence. Produce within us the ability to do what under the law we could never do ourselves. Enable us to love in the power of the Spirit and to demonstrate the fruit of the Spirit. We owe a debt we cannot pay; Jesus paid the debt He did not owe. Thank You, Jesus, for washing our sins away so we could sing a brand-new song. Amazing grace, how sweet the sound!

Living in Troubled Times
(From Psalm 119:25–34, 49-50)

Father, the past few years have been ones of grief over our children, our nation, and the world. Years in which we needed to cling to You and Your sovereignty over the affairs of men. Years in which a virus and violence have changed our nation.

It is our desire that our children would be like the sons of Issachar—that they would understand the times and know what to do and how to live. I pray for a revival in their hearts by the power of Your living Word so that their eyes would be opened to the deceptions of our days and the wickedness in our nation. May the truth of Your Word be written on their hearts and minds and transform their understanding of our nation and world.

We pray that You would take the blinders off their eyes so that they may see clearly and be able to judge rightly. May their ears be opened to hear the truth and may their hearts be softened to receive it. May they be lights in their darkened generation.

We ask that You would search them and know their hearts, know their anxious thoughts, see if there is any sinful way in them, and lead them in the everlasting way.

Our souls weep because of grief and cleave to the dust. Strengthen us according to Your Word. We have confessed our sins, and You have answered us with forgiveness. Graciously grant us the ability to walk in Your ways. We cling to You and Your testimonies; O Lord, do not put us to shame! Enlarge our hearts so that we may observe Your law and keep it with our whole hearts. Remember Your Word to Your servants in which You have made us hope. This is our comfort in our afflictions, that Your Word has revived us.

Affliction that Leads to Repentance

Therefore, brothers, since we have confidence to enter the holy places by the blood of Jesus, by the new and living way that he opened for us through the curtain, that is, through his flesh, and since we have a great priest over the house of God, let us draw near with a true heart in full assurance of faith, with our hearts sprinkled clean from an evil conscience and our bodies washed with pure water. Let us hold fast the confession of our hope without wavering, for he who promised is faithful (Hebrews 10:19–23).

Father, we come before Your throne of grace in the name of our Savior Jesus Christ. We come boldly and with confidence because Jesus is our Great High Priest whose own blood was poured out for us so that we may draw near with sincere hearts and full assurance of faith.

We have trusted in You and have told our children of Your glorious deeds, Your might, and the wonders that You have done.

We taught our children so that they might know You and arise and tell their children that they should set their hope in God and not forget the works of God but keep his commandments. But our children have become a stubborn and rebellious generation.

Oh, that their hearts would be inclined to always fear

You and keep all of Your commandments so that it might go well with them and with their descendants forever! (Deuteronomy 5:29)

Our hearts long for them to know, love, and serve You. But we know that You long for them even more. It is an honor and privilege to bring these names before Your throne. We may be the only ones bringing their names before You.

May they taste and see that You are good and realize that You have been patient and merciful to them. May they be drawn back into the faith and the fellowship of believers. We pray that they would long for You and cling to You and Your Word. We pray that You would give them a fear of You so that they may reverence You and desire to serve You with their whole hearts.

We pray that these prodigals would put away all malice, deceit, hypocrisy, envy, and slander. May they long for pure spiritual milk and grow up into salvation (1 Peter 2:1–5, 9–11). Some of these may never have been saved, though they may have grown up in church and have been taught Your ways. Only You know, but we can see the fruit of their lives and we know that they are not seeking after You.

We pray that our loved ones would be reminded of Your holiness. May they see themselves as You see them—lost in their sin and in need of salvation. These prodigals need to see themselves as sinners separated from

You. Open their eyes that they may behold wonderful things from Your law. May their souls be crushed with longing for You and Your ordinances. Rebuke them, for they have wandered from Your precepts. May Your precepts, laws, testimonies, and commandments be their counselors. Revive them according to Your Word and make them understand Your precepts.

Strengthen us as we pray for them, for our souls weep in our grief over them. Teach them Your statutes so that they may observe them. Give them understanding so that they may observe Your law and keep it with their whole hearts. Make them walk in the path of Your commandments. May they delight in Your testimonies. Turn their hearts away from the vanities of this world.

Lord, we do not want them to be afflicted, but we know that it is good to be afflicted so that they may learn Your statutes, for You use trials and tribulations to bring people to their knees. May they be afflicted in such a way that they will look to You and have hope. Be gracious to them so that they may consider their ways and turn their feet to Your commandments. In faithfulness afflict them so that Your loving kindness and compassion may comfort them.

O Lord, how we love Your Word. Give our prodigals a love for Your Word. May it be their meditation all the day. Make them wiser than their enemies. May they have more understanding than all their teachers. May Your testimonies be their meditation. Hold back their feet from every evil way in order that they may keep Your Word. Help them not to turn aside from Your rules as You have taught us. May Your words be sweeter than honey to them. May they have understanding to hate every false way.

May Your Word be a lamp to their feet and a light to their path. Hold their lives continually in Your hand so that they may no longer stray from Your precepts. May Your testimonies be their heritage forever and the joy of their hearts. Incline their hearts to perform Your statutes.

May they hate the double-minded but love Your law. May You be their hiding place and shield, and may they hope in Your Word. We ask that evildoers would depart from them so that they may keep Your commandments. Uphold these loved ones according to Your promise so that they may live and not be put to shame. Hold them up so that they may be safe and have regard for Your statutes continually! May their flesh tremble for fear of You, and may they be afraid of Your judgments. May Your Word be very near to them, in their hearts and in their mouths, so that they may hold fast to You and choose life by loving You and obeying You. May this be their life and their length of days.

And Father, we ask in the name of Jesus that You would strengthen and encourage us by the comfort of Your Spirit so that we may we trust in You absolutely as we look forward with great expectation to what You will do in answer to our prayers.

The "I AM" Statements of Jesus

God said to Moses, "I AM WHO I AM." And He said, "Say this to the people of Israel: 'I AM has sent me to you'" (Exodus 3:14).

Father, we come before You, the great "I AM." This is Your name forever and how You are to be remembered from generation to generation. We come boldly to this holy place, Your throne room, because You have given us access through the blood of Jesus. We have no merit in ourselves that would justify us before You. You have no reason to grant us an audience. You do so on the basis of our faith in Christ. We bring before You an offering of praise and thanksgiving for all that You have done for us. Thank You, dear Jesus, for humbling Yourself and willingly leaving the glories of heaven to be the sacrifice that satisfied the wrath of God. We have no words to fully express our gratitude. We are in awe of You. Thank You for giving us the privilege to come before You and pray. May we draw near today with sincere hearts full of faith.

We lift up our prodigals to You. May they be overwhelmed by Your presence. Give them an awareness of Your holiness. Remind them that they are but dust, yet You care for them. You are aware of every step they take and every word they speak, and You understand their thoughts from afar. Remind them that they cannot flee from Your Spirit. We ask that Your hand will lay hold of them and lead them in the paths of righteousness for Your name's sake. Search them and know their hearts and their anxious thoughts. Show them where they have been led astray and lead them in the everlasting way.

Jesus said to them, "I am the bread of life; whoever comes to me shall not hunger, and whoever believes in me shall never thirst (John 6:35).

We thank You, Jesus, that You are the living bread that has come down from heaven. You sustain us physically, emotionally, and spiritually. Our prodigals need the sustenance that only You can give. May You give them a hunger and thirst for righteousness. May they never be satisfied by this world. Stir up an insatiable longing within them that can be satisfied only by living bread and living water. May their hunger and thirst drive them to their knees to seek after You. May You save forever those who draw near to You.

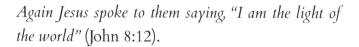

Again Jesus spoke to them saying, "I am the light of the world" (John 8:12).

Light cannot be overcome by darkness but rather dispels darkness. We live in a dark, sinful world. Our prodigals are blinded and living in darkness. They can't see to find their way out. Shine Your light on them and give them light for their path out of the darkness. Open their eyes and take the blinders off so that they can see clearly to follow You. May the warmth of Your light and Your love surround them and melt their stone-cold hearts. We ask that You would transfer them from the kingdom of darkness into Your kingdom of light.

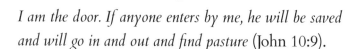

I am the door. If anyone enters by me, he will be saved and will go in and out and find pasture (John 10:9).

The world proclaims that there are other doors to eternal life, but we know that all must come through the one door, Jesus Christ. May our prodigals not bypass this door for all the other enticing ones out there. They have been and currently are tempted by the Vanity Fair of this life with so many ways to fulfill themselves and their dreams. But what they really need is the fresh green pastures of Your provision. They are blinded to their own enslavement to sin. Set them free and lead them to the door so that they may be saved and walk in the freedom of life with Christ.

I am the good shepherd. The good shepherd lays down his life for the sheep (John 10:11).

All we like sheep have gone astray. Each one of us has turned to our own way. Our way leads to death, yet we continue on that way just like wayward sheep who must be rescued by the shepherd. Our prodigals are like stubborn, wayward sheep. Or perhaps they are tormented by the pesky flies and gnats of Satan's lies. They are quick to follow the crowd even if they are heading for the cliff. But Your sheep know their good Shepherd and hear Your voice.

Some of these prodigals have made a profession of faith. Only You know if they are of Your flock. If so, Lord, they have gone astray and need You to leave the 99 and go find them. How we thank You that You have a heart for those who willfully stray, those who are tormented, those who just follow the crowd. We know that You may need to use Your rod of correction, and we trust that You will do so in mercy and with grace and great patience. May Your staff guide them into Your fold, where they may find rest for their souls. May Your goodness and mercy follow them all the days of their lives, and may they dwell in the house of the Lord forever.

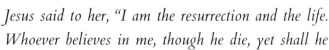

Jesus said to her, "I am the resurrection and the life. Whoever believes in me, though he die, yet shall he live, and everyone who lives and believes in me shall never die" (John 11:25–26).

Jesus, You are the resurrection and the life. The same power that raised You from the dead resides in us. May we become more aware of this reality day by day so that we may walk in light of this glorious truth. May those who see us recognize that we have been with You and be compelled to ask us about the hope that we have. And may our prodigals see that we believe in You and have abundant life because of You.

May they be drawn to us, not because of our good works but because they see that we have a living hope, a vibrant faith, and peace that surpasses understanding. We cannot produce this in ourselves. It is the outflow of our daily walk with You. Fill us with life so that it may flow through us and draw our prodigals and others to You.

Jesus said to him, "I am the way, and the truth, and the life. No one comes to the Father except through me" (John 14:6).

The world proclaims that there are many ways to God. Our prodigals believe this or choose not to believe in You at all. They go their own way, believe their own truth, and live their own lives completely independent of You. Show them that their ways are crooked and lead to destruction. Give them a revelation of Christ in all His glory so that they may receive life and someday stand before the Father righteous because they have been covered by the blood of Jesus.

I am the vine; you are the branches. Whoever abides in me and I in him, he it is that bears much fruit, for apart from me you can do nothing (John 15:5).

Apart from You, we can do nothing. Apart from You, nothing of eternal value happens. We must be connected to the vine and remain in You. We must abide in You day to day so that we may bear fruit and have our fruit remain. We grieve that much of our "fruit" does not remain. It was of our flesh and strength. Forgive us for walking in our own ways, thinking we were serving You. May Your grace and mercy cover years of unfruitful ministry and bring to life what seems dead.

May Your Word that has gone forth not come back to You void. May Your Word fulfill its purpose in the lives of our prodigals and be living and active in them, piercing the division between their hearts and souls. Judge the thoughts and intentions of their hearts. Do not cast them aside, but have mercy on their souls. Rescue them. Graft our prodigals into Your vine so that they may be holy and blameless before You and their lives may bear good fruit that will remain.

NOTES

NOTES